Unsolved!

MYSTERIES OF UFOS

Kathryn Walker

based on original text by Brian Innes

Crabtree Publishing Company

www.crabtreebooks.com

Crabtree Publishing Company

www.crabtreebooks.com

Author: Kathryn Walker
  based on original text by Brian Innes
Project editor: Kathryn Walker
Picture researcher: Rachel Tisdale
Managing editor: Miranda Smith
Art director: Jeni Child
Design manager: David Poole
Editorial director: Lindsey Lowe
Children's publisher: Anne O'Daly
Editor: Molly Aloian
Proofreaders: Ellen Rodger, Crystal Sikkens
Project coordinator: Robert Walker
Production coordinator: Katherine Kantor
Prepress technician: Katherine Kantor

This edition published in 2009 by
Crabtree Publishing Company

The Brown Reference Group plc
First Floor
9-17 St. Albans Place
London N1 0NX
www.brownreference.com

Copyright © 2008 The Brown Reference Group plc

Photographs:
Corbis: Columbia Pictures/ZUMA: p. 22–23
Fortean Picture Library: p. 6–7, 10–11, 16, 18–19,
  20, 24, 25, 26–27, 28
Istockphoto: Michael Knight: p. 17, 27 (insert);
  Paul LeFevre: p. 30
Mary Evans Picture Library: p. 4–5, 8, 12, 13,
  14–15, 21
NASA: Koen Miskotte, Dutch Meteor Society,
  Harderwijk, the Netherlands: p. 9
Superstock: cover
U. S. Department of Defense/U.S. Air Force:
  p. 28 (insert), 29

Every effort has been made to trace the
owners of copyrighted material.

Library and Archives Canada Cataloguing in Publication

Walker, Kathryn, 1957-
  Mysteries of UFOs / Kathryn Walker based on original text by Brian Innes.

(Unsolved!)
Includes index.
ISBN 978-0-7787-4145-9 (bound).--ISBN 978-0-7787-4158-9 (pbk.)

    1. Unidentified flying objects--Juvenile literature. I. Innes, Brian
II. Title. III. Series: Unsolved! (St. Catharines, Ont.)

TL789.2.W34 2008   j001.942   C2008-904328-6

Library of Congress Cataloging-in-Publication Data

Walker, Kathryn.
  Mysteries of UFOs / Kathryn Walker based on original text by Brian Innes.
    p. cm. -- (Unsolved!)
  Includes index.
  ISBN-13: 978-0-7787-4158-9 (pbk. : alk. paper)
  ISBN-10: 0-7787-4158-3 (pbk. : alk. paper)
  ISBN-13: 978-0-7787-4145-9 (lib. bdg. : alk. paper)
  ISBN-10: 0-7787-4145-1 (lib. bdg. : alk. paper)
  1. Unidentified flying objects--Juvenile literature. I. Innes, Brian. II. Title. III. Series.

TL789.2.W35 2009
001.942--dc22

                2008030105

Crabtree Publishing Company

Published in Canada
Crabtree Publishing
616 Welland Ave.
St. Catharines, ON
L2M 5V6

Published in the United States
Crabtree Publishing
PMB16A
350 Fifth Ave., Suite 3308
New York, NY 10118

Contents

The Roswell Incident

...People started to see flying saucers in the 1940s.

The Foster ranch was in New Mexico. Mac Brazel lived there. On June 13, 1947, there was a storm. Mac said he heard an explosion. The next morning he found strange wreckage on his ranch.

It looked like tinfoil but it was very strong. Mac could not tear it. On July 5, Mac heard that people had seen "flying saucers" in the sky. He reported his find to the **USAAF** base in Roswell.

On July 8, Major Jesse Marcel came to take away the wreckage. He said it was like "nothing made on Earth." But later, the Air Force said that the metal was from a **weather balloon**.

>> **USAAF** — United States Army Air Force

Mac Brazel shows the metal that he found on his ranch. He thought it was from a flying saucer.

"...Major Jesse Marcel ...said it was like nothing made on Earth."

On July 8, 1947, there was another strange incident. Grady L. Barnett was in the desert of New Mexico. He saw something on the ground. He thought that it might be an aircraft that had crashed.

Grady hurried over to the wreckage. He said it looked like "some sort of metallic, disk-shaped object." A group of students had been working nearby. They joined Grady.

Dead Aliens?

There were some bodies near the wreckage! Grady said they looked like humans. But they were not humans. The heads were round and large. The eyes were small. There was no hair on their heads. They wore gray coveralls.

The Army arrived and roped off the area. They told Grady and the others not to tell anyone about what they had seen.

"...they looked like humans. But they were not humans."

*This is a display from the UFO museum in Roswell, New Mexico. It shows a scientist examining a dead **alien** from the craft that crashed in 1947.*

>> **alien** — A creature from another planet

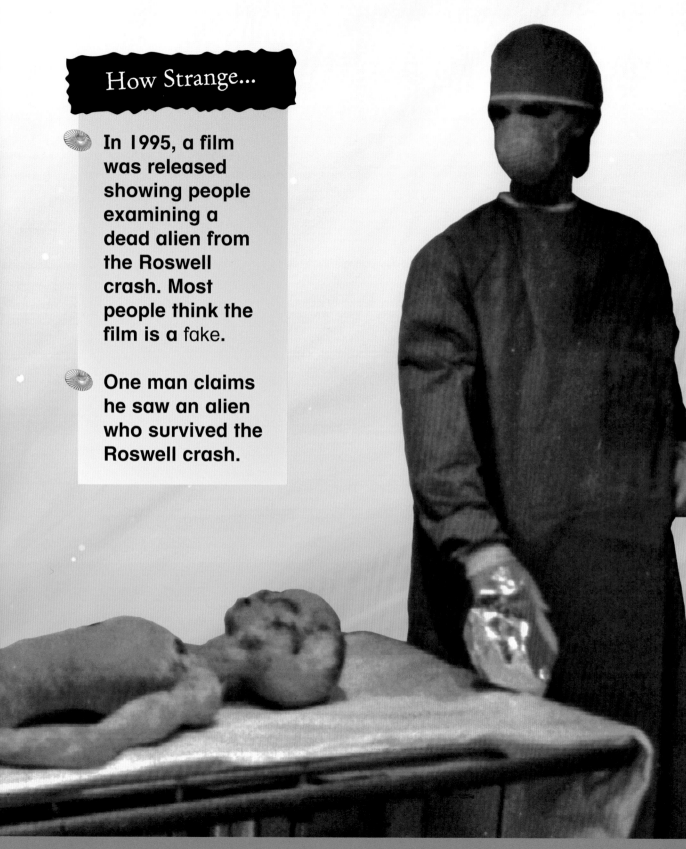

How Strange...

- **In 1995, a film was released showing people examining a dead alien from the Roswell crash. Most people think the film is a** fake.

- **One man claims he saw an alien who survived the Roswell crash.**

Many people thought that the two events in New Mexico were linked. Together, they became known as the Roswell Incident.

The U.S. Navy experimented with this balloon in 1949. Maybe the wreckage that Mac Brazel found in 1947 came from a similar balloon.

Project Mogul

In 1994, the Air Force said that a top secret project began in 1947. It was named Project Mogul. The project used high-flying balloons to spy on the **Soviet Union**. The Air Force said the wreckage had come from one of the balloons.

>> **Soviet Union** — Formerly, a large country in eastern Europe and northern Asia

Many people still think that the wreckage was from an alien spacecraft. They believe that alien bodies were found in the desert. The Air Force said that these 'bodies' were test dummies, used in an experiment.

UFO Sightings

At the time of the Roswell Incident, a lot of people reported seeing "flying saucers" in the sky. The flying saucers soon became known as "**Unidentified Flying Objects**" (UFOs).

"Many UFOs can be identified or explained."

This is a meteor falling through the sky. People have sometimes mistaken meteors *for UFOs.*

Many UFOs can be identified or explained. They are often balloons or meteors. A meteor is a piece of rock or metal that travels through space. It burns up as it falls toward Earth. Some say there is a natural explanation for all UFOs. But some sightings are hard to explain.

Mysteries in the Skies

...Throughout history people have seen strange objects in the sky.

On April 4, 1561, something **astonishing** happened above the city of Nuremberg in Germany. People wrote about what they saw.

There were huge black tubes in the sky. Colored **globes** came out of them. Crosses, disks, and other shapes appeared, too. Many people watched this strange event.

People said it was as if the objects were fighting a fierce battle in the sky. It lasted for about one hour. Some of the objects flew off into the Sun. Others crashed and vanished in smoke.

>> **astonishing** — Something amazing or impressive

This picture shows what people saw in the sky above Nuremburg on April 4, 1561.

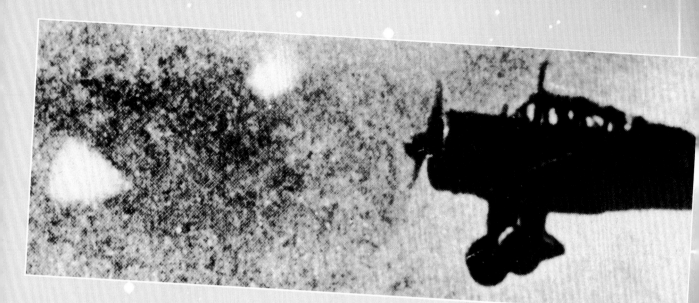

Foo Fighters

During World War II, pilots in Europe and the Pacific reported seeing strange lights in the sky.

*This photograph was taken in 1945. It shows a Japanese **fighter** plane with two foo fighters.*

Balls of light would suddenly appear out of nowhere. They would dart around the sky. It was as if they were playing with the aircraft. U.S. pilots named them "foo fighters."

The pilots thought that the foo fighters were a German secret weapon. But these balls of light did not harm any of the planes.

After the war, German pilots said that they had seen the balls of light, too. The Germans had thought they were a U.S. secret weapon!

>> **fighter** — A plane designed to destroy enemy aircraft in the air

Photographs of a UFO

Paul Trent was a farmer. He lived with his wife near McMinnville in Oregon. On May 11, 1950, Paul and his wife saw a silvery disk in the sky. They took two photographs of it.

A local newspaper printed the photographs. Some people thought the photographs were fakes. They said that the Trents had taken pictures of a **model** hung from a string. Much later, experts examined the photographs. They decided that the Trents' photographs were real.

"...experts... decided that the Trents' photographs were real."

Evelyn Trent took this photograph of a UFO in Oregon on May 11, 1950.

>> **model** — A small copy of an object

Project Blue Book

...In 1952, the U.S. Air Force had 1,500 new reports of UFO sightings.

The Air Force created "Project Blue Book" to check out these sightings. In its first year, Project Blue Book was very busy.

During the month of July 1952, many people reported seeing UFOs over Washington D.C. Glowing objects were spotted over the White House and the Capitol building. These unknown objects also showed up on **radar** screens in the area. Radar is equipment used for finding distant objects. It can show where objects are and how fast they are traveling.

Some time later, Project Blue Book said unusual weather conditions had caused lights in the sky. They said that these conditions had caused the **blips** on the radar screens, too.

How Strange...

There were 150 reports of UFOs in June 1952. Before that there had been fewer than 20 each month.

There were 536 reports of UFOs in July 1952. Fifty of these were on just one day.

>> **radar** — A device that uses radio waves to locate an object

This is an artists idea of the scene at Andrews Air Force Base on July 26, 1952. On this day, UFOs were spotted at the base near Washington, D.C.

insert

It was July 17, 1957. An Air Force **bomber** was flying from Mississippi into Oklahoma. During the flight, the **crew** saw a bright blue-white light. It was racing at high speed toward them.

Chase in the Skies

The light looked as if it was going to hit the plane. Suddenly the light changed direction and disappeared. Later, the pilot said that the light had been "as big as a barn."

Ground control saw the object on their radar screens. They gave the bomber permission to chase it. The bomber chased the UFO for 700 miles (1,126 km). Then the UFO vanished.

In 1957, a UFO was spotted following this B-47 jet bomber. An arrow marks the position of the UFO. In the insert box on the left, you can see the UFO up close.

>> **bomber** — An aircraft that drops bombs

The Air Force and Project Blue Book agreed about the UFO. They said that the object seen over Dallas and Fort Worth had been a passenger plane. Many people did not think that this could explain what happened that day.

Blue Book Closes

There were thousands of UFO reports over the years. Project Blue Book could not look into all of them. In 1969, Blue Book closed down.

"There were thousands of UFO reports over the years."

This is an artists idea of what a flying saucer looks like. People have often described seeing UFOs that look like these.

Close Encounters

...Some people claim to have had close contact with UFOs.

Dr. J. Allen Hynek felt that there was not enough scientific **investigation** into UFOs. In 1973, he set up the Center for UFO Studies.

Dr. Hynek sorted UFO sightings into groups. If someone saw a UFO less than 500 feet (152 meters) away, he called it a "close **encounter**." There were three types of close encounters:

- Close Encounters of the First Kind— When people clearly see a UFO.
- Close Encounters of the Second Kind— When the UFO has an effect on surroundings, people, or animals. For example, it might leave a mark on the ground.
- Close Encounters of the Third Kind— When beings (living creatures) are seen in or near UFOs.

>> **investigation** — The process of trying to find out all the facts

Some motorists have described Close Encounters of the Second Kind. They say their cars stopped working while UFOs have passed or hovered above them.

The man on the left side of this picture is George Adamski. He claimed to have met with aliens and traveled on their spaceships.

There have been many reports of Close Encounters of the Third Kind. This is when people see beings that have come from a UFO.

Visitor From Venus?

George Adamski reported a strange meeting in the California desert. It happened on November 20, 1952. George said he saw a UFO land. Then he met with an alien from the planet **Venus**.

George later said that he was allowed to travel in flying saucers. He claimed to have visited Venus and other planets.

How Strange...

- Some people claim to have been kidnapped by aliens.

- In many of these cases, people say the aliens did medical tests on them.

>> **Venus** — The second planet from the Sun in our solar system.

UFO at the Mission

Reverend William Gill was a **missionary**. He was based in Papua New Guinea. This is a country in the southwest Pacific Ocean.

On June 26, 1959, Reverend Gill saw an object like a flying disk. It came toward his mission house. Gill watched it with 37 other people. They saw four figures appear on top of the object. Then it vanished.

The following evening the UFO returned. The figures appeared again. Reverend Gill raised his arm and waved. The figure waved back. One of Reverend Gill's companions waved both arms. Two of the figures did the same!

On the third night, eight objects appeared high in the sky. Afterward, everything returned to normal at the mission house.

In June 1959, people in Papua New Guinea saw figures waving from a disk-shaped flying object.

"They saw four figures appear on top of the object."

Men in black

...People who report seeing UFOs sometimes have strange visitors.

Albert Bender lived in Connecticut. He produced a UFO magazine. In 1953, Albert announced "I know what the saucers are!" He planned to print what he had found out in his magazine. But first he mailed his report to a friend.

A few days later Albert claimed that three men entered his bedroom. They were dressed in black and wore hats. Albert said that their eyes "suddenly lit up like flashlight bulbs."

One of the men told Albert his report was true. But he ordered Albert not to tell anyone the truth. He told him to stop producing his magazine. Albert did what he was told. He said he had been "scared to death" by the men in black.

How Strange...

- Men in black look and dress like old movie characters named G-men. The G-men were FBI agents.

- Men in black are often said to move in a stiff and awkward way.

This is a picture from the 1997 comedy movie Men in Black. Unlike these movie characters, the men in black that have visited people are very frightening.

A Scary Meeting

Robert Richardson lived in Toledo, Ohio. In July 1967, he crashed his car into a strange object. The object was blocking the road. Robert thought it was a UFO. Almost immediately, the object vanished. But Robert found a small piece of metal on the road.

One week later, two men came to Robert's home. They were dressed in black suits. The men asked Robert for the piece of metal. Robert told them he had sent it away to be examined. The men then threatened to harm Robert's wife if he didn't get the metal back.

Threats

In 1975, Carlos de Los Santos Montiel was driving to a television studio in Mexico. He planned to talk about some UFOs he had seen.

Two black **limousines** forced Carlos to stop his car. Men in black suits got out. One of them told Carlos, "Don't talk any more about this sighting of yours." They threatened to harm him and his family if he talked about the UFOs.

In 1953, Albert Bender was threatened by three men in black. This is a sketch that Albert made of one of the men who visited his home.

>> **limousine** — A large and luxurious car

Aliens?

Governments say that the men in black are not working for them or for the **military**. If this is true, then perhaps people are making up these stories. Or maybe the strangers are not human. Some people believe that the men in black are aliens.

"...maybe the strangers are not human."

Could the mysterious men in black be aliens who are trying to look like humans?

What is the Truth?

...Many UFO sightings can be explained. A few remain a mystery.

For centuries, people have reported seeing strange objects in the sky. Some of the reports were sightings of meteors or planets. Some were strange cloud formations. Others were found to be **hoaxes**.

In the late 1800s and early 1900s, people discovered that some of the strange objects were airships. Airships were a new type of aircraft.

In more recent times, people have reported seeing UFOs that moved very fast. These may be new planes or weapons that are being tested. They may need to be kept secret.

How Strange...

- During World War II, Germany was experimenting with disk-shaped aircraft.

- One of these "flying disks" could travel at speeds of almost 1,250 miles per hour (2,011 km per hour).

- In the 1950s the Avro Aircraft Company built a disk-shaped aircraft.

>> **hoax** — A trick

These strange cloud formations are known as **lenticular** clouds. The insert panel (right) shows an artists idea of a flying saucer. It is easy to see how lenticular clouds could be mistaken for flying saucers.

>> **lenticular** — Lentil-shaped, by being curved outward on both sides

The Lubbock Lights

On August 25, 1951, a group of scientists in Lubbock, Texas saw a **formation** of blue lights in the sky. Over the next few weeks, they saw similar groups of lights. On August 31, a student named Carl Hart took a photograph of them.

Some people thought that the lights came from a new type of jet bomber. This plane was called the Northrop YB-49. It was flat and V-shaped. As a result, it was known as the "flying wing."

"...a group of scientists...saw a formation of blue lights in the sky."

Below is a photograph that Carl Hart took of the Lubbock Lights. The aircraft on the right is the Northrop YB-49 jet. Could it have been the source of the lights?

>> **formation** — An arrangement or group of things or people.

Top Secret

The F-117A Stealth fighter aircraft was developed in secret. It first flew in 1981. But the Air Force kept the aircraft secret until 1988.

The Stealth fighter was designed to be difficult to see or **locate**. It is low and black with a batwing shape. Its unusual shape makes it look like a flying saucer during flight. At a time when the Stealth fighter was still a secret, it might have been mistaken for a flying saucer.

This is an F-117A Stealth fighter plane. Work began on the airplane in 1976, but it was a well-kept secret for many years.

>> **locate** — To discover or find out where something is

It is possible that new types of aircraft have been mistaken for UFOs. Some reports of UFO sightings have turned out to be hoaxes. But this does not explain all UFOs across the world. Were the others imagined or real? Do UFOs really come from other worlds?

Some people have suggested that aliens could come from this group of stars. It is named the Pleiades. But an astronaut from Earth would take nearly seven million years to reach them.

Alien Visitors?

Space exploration has uncovered the major planets in our **solar system**. People only know about life on Earth. Some people think that UFOs come from farther out in space. Maybe aliens have found ways of traveling these huge distances.

Most scientists think that UFOs are imaginary. But many people all over the world claim to have seen UFOs. To these people, the UFOs seem real. They wonder if UFOs could be spaceships from other worlds.

Glossary

agent Someone who represents a government organization

alien A creature from another planet

astonishing Something amazing or impressive

blip A spot seen on a radar screen that shows the position of an object

bomber An aircraft that drops bombs

crew People working on board an aircraft or ship

encounter An unexpected meeting with somebody or something

FBI Federal Bureau of Investigation

fake Something that is not what it seems to be, but is intended to trick people

fighter A plane designed to destroy enemy aircraft in the air

formation An arrangement or group

globe Anything round and shaped like a ball

hoax A trick

investigation The process of trying to find out all the facts

lenticular Lentil-shaped, by being curved outward on both sides

limousine A large and luxurious car

locate To discover or find out where something is

military The armed forces of a country

missionary A person who is sent to an area to do religious work

model A small copy of an object

radar A device that uses radio waves to locate an object

solar system The Sun and the planets that move around it

Soviet Union Formerly, a large country in eastern Europe and northern Asia

unidentified When you do not know what something is

USAAF United States Army Air Force

Venus The second planet from the Sun in our solar system

weather balloon A balloon that carries equipment for gathering weather information

Index

Further Reading

- Grace, N.B. *UFOs: What Scientists Say May Shock You!*, "24/7: Science Behind the Scenes" series. Franklin Watts, 2008.
- Krull, Kathleen. *What Really Happened in Roswell?* HarperTrophy, 2003.
- Oxlade, Chris. *The Mystery of UFOs*, "Can Science Solve?" series. Heinemann Library, 2006.
- Sievert, Terri. *UFOs,* "The Unexplained" series. Edge Books, 2004.
- Tiger, Caroline. *The UFO Hunter's Handbook*, "Field Guides to the Paranormal" series. Price Stern Sloan, 2001.

Printed in the U.S.A.